PRAISE FOR *MUD-WRESTLING* . . .

"Writers who invite us not simply to accompany their spiritual journey but to enter it with them run the risk of sentimentality. The honesty branding the stories of Sean's muddy wrestling avoids that trap with grace at every turn. All short pieces here (poems, sketches, tales) were 'muscled onto the page' by one man's hunger for truth and his desire to share with other seekers. This book will meet you right where you are. Be prepared for a takedown: the grace is in the mud."

REVEREND AUSTIN FLEMING
Pastor, Holy Family Church
Concord, Massachusetts

"The whole spectrum of the inner life is here, in a uniquely male expression, from primal impulses bordering on insanity to divine revelation, embodied in one person's life and words. Read this book to face the parts of yourself that you want to know and the parts you've been trying to avoid, and most especially to discover that there is more to you than you ever dreamed possible."

SWAMI NIRMALANANDA
Svaroopa Vidya Ashram

"Sean tells it straight, writing from the heart. He dares us to notice our wounded yet wonderful lives and to love ourselves even if it means feeling a big ache inside. His book is a shot of adrenaline, a wake-up call, a strong loving hand steady at your back."

JAY W. VOGT
Author of *Recharge Your Team:*
The Grounded Visioning Approach

"Behind Sean LeClaire's sometimes acerbic, sometimes edgy, hilarious, frank, tender portrayal of the vicissitudes of our wayward minds lies a deep compassion for human suffering, particularly that of men, himself included, and a clear and compelling vision of the magnificent beings we men could be, and occasionally are. This book is sacred text."

THOMAS YEOMANS, Ph.D.
Director, Concord Institute

"We often can hear our own patterns more easily by listening intimately to another. In *Mud-Wrestling with My Mind*, Sean allows this to happen by sharing honestly and generously his most intimate thoughts and the timeless wisdom born of his journey."

NAN SHAW
Author of *How to Get Your Wiggle Back!*

"When a man who is tougher than most and once was angrier than most opens his heart and tells the world through wonderfully written essays and poems his journey to self-transformation, it is an opportunity not to be missed. Sean is a gifted writer and teacher who shares his personal experience, not theory, with us."

FRED L. MILLER
Author of *How to Calm Down Even
If You're Absolutely, Totally Nuts*

Mud-Wrestling with My Mind

The Fine Art of Acceptance

Sean Casey LeClaire

RED SPIRAL BOOKS
CONCORD, MASSACHUSETTS

Red Spiral Books
PO Box 1354
West Concord Station
Concord, MA 01742
http://www.seanleclaire.com

Cover, book design, and typography:
Carolyn Kasper and Dede Cummings, dcdesign

Copyright © 2011 by Sean Casey LeClaire

All rights reserved. No part of this publication may be reproduced in any form whatsoever without written permission from the publisher, except for brief quotations embodied in literary articles or reviews.

Printed in the United States of America

Publisher's Cataloging-in-Publication Data
LeClaire, Sean Casey.

Mud-wrestling with my mind : the fine art of acceptance / Sean Casey LeClaire. — Concord, Mass. : Red Spiral Books, c2011.

p. ; cm.

ISBN: 978-0-9724859-1-3
Summary: A collection of spiritual insights told through stories and poems revealing strategies for getting through the sludge of confusion and attaining clarity and deepened awareness in order to love and serve in the world.

1. LeClaire, Sean Casey. 2. Self-acceptance. 3. Self-perception. 4. Self-realization. 5. Spiritual biography. I. Title.

BF575.S37 L43 2011   2011912394
158.1—dc23   1110

1 3 5 7 9 10 8 6 4 2

Contents

Preface   xi

I. KNEE-DEEP IN MUD

Artist	3
Rant	7
Projection	10
Porn	13
Frank	15
Denial	19
Layers	20
Cars	21
Good	23
Opinions	24
The Cave	25
Son	28

II. TRUDGING

Parts	33
Heed	35
Support	37
The Brush	39
Eddie Brown	45
The Image	47
Birds	49
Mud Tracks	50
Choice	51
Tough	53
Resistance	55

III. FOOTWORK

Hired	61
Sweet	65
Perception	67
Roles	68
Oranges	70
Cockroaches	72
Inner Star	74
Reality	76
Baby Jesus	77
The Scooter	82
On the Altar	85
Things I've Learned	86

IV. A FLOWER RISES

Conundrum	89
Om!	90
The Dog	93
Standing in Love	95
More on Love	96
The Talk	98
The Key	100
Yoga	102
The Call	103
Acceptance	105
Illumination	107
Being	108
Old Man	109
Afterword	111

Teachers are like trees. Teachers show us how to sink our roots deep in the earth. They give shade and cover when things get too hot or too wet. And they help students branch out so the light can shine through.

Mud-Wrestling with My Mind is dedicated to three redwoods I roll with:

Garbis Dimidjian
Swami Nirmalananda
Patrick Thornton

Only where love and need are one,
And the work is play for mortal stakes,
Is the deed ever really done
For Heaven and the future's sakes.

> Robert Frost
> From "Two Tramps in Mud Time"

PREFACE

The journey of spiritual awakening, which involves a struggle to overcome mind confusion and attain clarity and deeper awareness, is perhaps most aptly symbolized by one of the most exquisite flowers in the world—the lotus, which rises from roots in the mud of a swamp or pond to flower on the placid, clear water surface.

Despite the good intentions of the majority of individuals, I agree with the mad Russian writer Dostoyevsky when he wrote in the parable of the Grand Inquisitor, told in the *Brothers Karamazov*, that most of humanity just wants authority, mystery, and miracles. Nevertheless, a growing number of people want something more substantial and profound than the self-serving charisma and superficial leadership that is pervasive throughout our world today. Such people want inner peace, real connection, and a deeper sense of purpose. They want to rise out of the mud in order to shine and serve the world. I wrote *Mud* for such folks.

Mud-Wrestling with My Mind, like my first book, *Hug an Angry Man,* is for men and women who continue to mud-wrestle with their minds to better integrate and understand the multidimensionality of their being. I have trudged knee-deep in the muddy confusion of my own mind, wrestling with it constantly, and like all people who stay the course, I am opening to the timeless wisdom of the self—the light and love we are made of.

Happy mud-wrestling, and enjoy the beauty of who you really are—an amazing flower planted on this little blue planet, third from the sun.

– 1 –
KNEE-DEEP IN MUD

There's courage involved if you want to become Truth.
— RUMI

ARTIST

"**Mommy says** writers can't make money."

"When did she say that?" I ask as my son leans on my shoulder while I stare at the empty, blinking computer screen.

"Mommy says writing plays is stupid." I give him *the look*, and off he goes, eager to play with the kids who live in the big yellow house down the street.

"Artists are the guardians of freedom!" I yell toward the back of the house.

"I know, Dad," my son answers as he descends the back stairs. "Can we go swimming at Walden's Pond later?"

I like what my son's second grade teacher said at orientation to a gathering of twenty or so parents. "If you will believe half of what your kids say happens at school, I will believe *half* of what the kids say happens at home!" Whether my ex said those things to our son is not something I dwell on. It's hard to shame an artist because we are pretty damn good at doing that to ourselves. Shame is pride turned inward. Pride kills writers. Shame buries them.

The economically minded and structured society we live in is not set up to support the artist's way. Regardless, I write most days, every morning five hundred words or until 9:00 a.m., whichever comes first. Then I do the leadership development and coaching work I enjoy.

What many of my coaching clients often misunderstand or refuse to accept is that development of a creative or artistic talent into a skill requires the hard work of honing one's craft. When it comes to creative endeavors we are either trained or untrained. Repetition is the mother of skill. This happens one day at a time—in my case, one word, one phrase, one sentence at a time. It is not about what you produce, but about making time for your craft and consistently showing up.

. . .

The computer screen remains empty. I'm drinking green tea, waiting for words to come, staring at the blank screen, *trying* to write. Writing is religion. I enjoy engaging memory, imagination, and inspiration—breathing in and onto the page, sitting in front of it in an alert, relaxed state, waiting for words to rise up from deep waters. Writing is like surfing: you wait for the slightest movement, an infinitesimal shift in the current, a ripple on the surface. Sometimes you wait all day, but when it comes there is *magic* and you ride the wave to the shore, or sometimes just splash about.

I notice a backpack filled with fifty-seven notebooks leaning against the wall by the window in my office, notebooks I lugged around the world for three years while living in Benedictine monasteries and yoga ashrams—wandering, wondering, and writing. Seeing the notebooks takes up space from which creation arises. Notebooks filled with words, images, sensations, feelings, impulses, and insights contained in drab, brown, flip-top, coiled steno pads like the kind you get for grade school, waiting to be shaped into sentences and paragraphs.

The notepads are getting under my skin, and I begin to pace. A blue jay snaps a monarch butterfly over the garden. I peek into my son's room, see stuff everywhere, and pick up a few things. Writing is easy, a writer once said. You just sit down in front of a blank page and wait till blood begins to form on your brow. If you want to write, you have to clear your mind, take one step forward and jump. Writing is work—a physical action—like wrestling a twenty-foot python or running steel on a railroad gang. I muscle a word onto the page.

I don't give a flying fuck about Hemingway and his damn sharpened pencils, or the fact that each day he stopped a story in the middle of a sentence, trusting that he'd begin right where he left off in the scene the next morning. I don't care about writing near a window, at night, or at the crack of dawn. I don't give a shit that Stephen King writes two thousand words *every day*. Imagine if that man didn't write. I don't care if the playwright Sam Shepard only writes when he feels passionate about an idea. Bully for him. My fingers strike keys . . . *Harvey had a face like a bad road.*

Now that sentence goes in easy, like a tongue licking its way up something silky, soft, wet, and sweet. I look over at the picture of Hemingway, which I picked up at his home in Key West while vacationing in Florida with my ex. The old man is fishing with an escape-to-the-horizon grin on his face. He was happy at sea and when he was writing.

"Hey, Papa, I'll get my words today!" I say out loud, flicking him the bird.

Where are my words going? I don't know, and I don't care. I'm writing, like surfing. *Harvey had a face like a bad road.*

I stop thinking about writing and write—grab a goddamn sentence, snap its neck, pound my fist into the table, crack my knuckles and a few sorry syllables spill out on the page. People like to think writers live a romantic lifestyle. Yeah, right! Writers, like all artists, go into dark corners, start kicking things around a bit, stir the pot, open closets where bones have been buried and forgotten. Artists say and present things that we don't like to talk about in polite society. Writers whistle while they burn.

Writing is not for the tenderhearted. Putting a paragraph together can be as calculating as an in-law giving you a cold shoulder at Thanksgiving dinner, or as stalemating as a three-year-old son simply refusing to do what you want him to do, or as mean-spirited as a spouse telling you, on your birthday, that they want a divorce. Happy birthday, honey! I've had words fly across my desk, turn, spin, and topple like teeth shattered from the blow of a lead pipe. I've followed words, phrases to the source of sound, only to become aware that all my fierce soul really wants to say that day is, "Where's my blanky?" Yet because I write to find beauty and truth, what moves me, what scares me, what I revere, for me it is a holy experience.

My son thumps upstairs and asks, "How's writing, Daddy?"

"Got my five hundred words. Let's go swimming!"

RANT

The next new age conehead who greets me with his silly "I honor the light in you" grin is gonna get a good solid smack in the eater! Self-help! Yoga! Buddhism! What's next, Deepak? Freeway billboards, maybe a Rinpoche Lexus. The whole damn thing's been co-opted by our monstrous American ego. There's just too many sick angry men hiding in the health food store aisles. New age sensitive guys. Hey! Hey! But I'm really not some throwback Neanderthal, one of those Promise Keepers promising to keep the little woman in the friggin' dark ages—no way, José. And I'm no politician promoting war, cowards, killing our brave young men, same as those slick corporate dickheads. I've had my fill of that bullshit. And I'm certainly not gonna go to another of those men's recruitment nights. Pheff!

I'm not sure about the men's movement. At one time in the '90s, it gathered some speed. At its peak, Bly, Meade, and Hillman got forty-eight thousand men to tromp into the woods, bang some drums, read a little poetry. Do you know how many divorced fathers there are in America? Twenty-four million. Do the math . . . the majority of men haven't even begun to scratch the surface of their lives.

I don't know about the men's movement. One Friday night, I'm standing in the dark watching grown men in a big circle in a forest. (What? Didn't these friggin' guys ever get to play in the woods when they were kids?) My roomie dragged me there, and about sixty other goombahs, being goaded, shamed into charging up with a sixteen-pound sledge and slamming a bell.

Join a men's team!

Like, we didn't get enough of that competitive crap when we were kids. No, let's do it all over again in our mid to late forties and fifties. Then the rah-rah leaders get the guys all revved up, and they run out into a field and start playing tackle football—on ice!

Now if it had been snow, I might have crushed some suckers . . . nothing like a good snow bowl. But ice! I'm painting two rooms in my new house tomorrow. I need my body for work. So this monkey standing beside me, taking a break from the ice football battle, looks down at me and says, "How come you're not out there, *pussy?*"

Now, where I come from we don't bother people we don't know. So I smash him up against a tree, grab his balls, squeeze, and reply, "Actually, I feel a little insecure, 'cause I'd like to play but I don't want to get hurt since I have to paint two rooms in my new house tomorrow. I think it's time for me to go home. What do you think?" The guy's face had turned purple, and he was having trouble breathing. I finally came to my senses, let go of his nuts, and headed out of the forest.

I'm not sure *how* to be the man I want to be. My reaction to that big rude fatty was wrong. I know that! I need a few more inches on my fuse. Anytime I'm angry, I know I'm frightened about something, real or imagined. Maybe I need to bang a few drums in the woods, but I'll be damned if I'm gonna do it with men who will hurt me, or hurt other men, ever again. I've had it with men's locker room intimacy, whether it's in the desert, a forest, a locker room, a coffee shop, or some bar . . . anywhere guys spit sports stats at each other and call it relating. You'll find your fair share of assholes anywhere—in boardrooms, ball courts, bedrooms—drowning in their own self-importance. Bullies . . . I don't like the bullies out there, and I don't like the bully in me!

I'm not sure how to be a real man, or . . . where to look for guidance. Who are our role models? Athletes? Many of them are nothing but overpaid babies. Actors? They change wives like soiled underwear. Those Hollywood boys oughta diaper that inner child of theirs. Politicians? Yeah, right! Priests? I don't think so! CEOs and Gurus? They've fallen.

What I do know is that being a man has something to do with self-respect and gentleness, power and softness. A woman once told me that is what they want, strong and gentle. But that won't cut it this time! I need to hear from men. What's going on in their balls, in their hearts! How they deal with stuff inside. I need to hear stories about love, about truth, about honor, about hurt, and how to get beyond it. I need to hear some shining stories.

I'm a long way from there. But I'm willing to begin, man!

PROJECTION

I had hated the guy.

My hate took the form of jealousy, with impulses to rip one of his arms off and beat him half to death with it. He was lean and tall, one of those new age sensitive guys—the sexy, slippery kind who would bed a best friend's wife. It didn't help that I imagined the guy had a thunder-cock that could fulfill any woman's sexual longing. I'd first encountered him at a spiritual retreat center where my beloved companion and I were taking a weekend workshop. He slinked over to where we were seated during lunch. They talked. I fumed inside. A few months later the guy appeared at a gathering for a Guru that my partner and I were attending. I made up some doozy imaginings about this guy and my woman. I think she barely knew he existed, and I didn't know the guy from Adam; but that didn't matter much, since my mind still tortured me with images that made me jealous.

Last summer the Guru came to town again. My companion offered loving service (*seva*) for the duration of the Guru's stay. I had let her know that I'd show up at the open evening for the public. But as evening approached, my mind created images of me punching the guy's lights out right in front of the Guru. I haven't read all the rules, but I don't think you are supposed to start fights at spiritual gatherings. As my fear-filled mind created its movie, making me feel jealous all afternoon, I became increasingly apprehensive about going.

So I prayed to the Guru for guidance—not something I was normally prone to do. I'll sit with Gurus, but praying to them, that's not for me. I've always thought they were nothing more than any other thing infused with light and love, which is everything. I can get as much from sitting in a field of wildflowers or watching my beloved working in her garden or listening to the giggle-glory of my five-year-old son as sitting with a Guru. And all the hoopla that goes on with many of their disciples I find childish. But since I felt frightened to go to the evening because I might hammer some guy, I prayed to the Guru then persuaded myself to go to the evening with my son.

There were over 2,500 people in the building, and who's right in front of me in the bloody line to get into the main hall? Yep, old thunder-cock himself, standing about eight feet away. This particular Guru apparently puts whatever you need to deal with right in your face when you pray to her. I turned and really looked at the man. Indeed, he was handsome in an awkward way, with a square jaw, bent nose, full lips, and a woman's shoulders, delicate lines. His eyes flitted from woman to woman in the line. The guy appeared needy, distracted, and nervous, as if "looking for Mommy." Suddenly a prayer of forgiveness formed in my mind. In that humbling moment, I remembered sleeping with a close friend's girlfriend when

I was seventeen, something I had never thought about since performing that drunken act.

Continuing to observe the man, I felt nothing but compassion, and I heard the Guru's voice in my heart, which I will remember forever. Standing there, I offered a blessing of peace to the man and bowed.

Then my son and I walked into the main room and sat awhile. I began to cry soft tears of surrender and self-forgiveness, while my son drew pictures of sunflowers in a notepad. The Guru came on stage. Although we were thirty yards away, I felt her looking directly at me, the way these weird and wonderful saints can do, and she smiled. I felt as free as a mountain breeze. Then my beloved companion walked toward me and my son. We kissed gently and went for dinner, the three of us holding hands.

PORN

It is interesting how I sometimes think about porn when I am completely calm, alone at home, my woman away again. The thought arises, *go to a porn site*. I don't use porn, had my fill of strip joints, peeler bars, and the like when I was a youth growing up in Montreal . . . the gentlemen's ballet capitol of the world. Now I know if you scratch lust you will inevitably find utter loneliness and if you can stay with the layers of the internal unfolding, then you eventually awaken—or at bare minimum, the qualities of what we call love become increasingly present in your life. *I wonder if God likes porn* . . . So I sit with the flickering thought of lust, and loneliness does arise. I learned a long time ago that you can't masturbate your way to peace, a fleeting moment of pleasure, sure, but lasting peace, no way. It doesn't work like that; otherwise, we'd see millions of peaceful men walking around, which, arguably, we do not.

Pornography is an addiction. Porn has proliferated, mutated, and gone underground because of the Web. Porn gives rise to the perception of power, pseudopower. False power separates and isolates. Using porn destroys trust, destroys marriages, and destroys your soul. According to statistics in America, six men in ten use some form of porn weekly. Porn is about powerlessness.

Many men feel powerless! A man comes home, sits in the dark, places his body in front of the pixel hell of a pulsating flat screen, stares into the plastic tit of fear, and covets the flesh of other men's daughters, as he pulls his John Henry or Mr. Happy or whatever he has named his penis. He has a genital fart, with absolutely no inner peace.

FRANK

He's in an aisle seat in first class on an afternoon flight from Los Angeles to New York. A bear of a man, a sales guy for Fox Network, he's talking baseball, booze, and broads—hopped up over some television program about people surviving on an island that has become a ratings miracle. Since leaving the business world, I no longer watch television, so I don't understand what he's talking about. For a long time I sit next to the guy, with a belly like a large bowl of grief, full of things half eaten and swallowed, and listen quietly, nodding, ahumming, and thinking about why I am going to New York: to meet with a literary agent about the possibility of getting a book published about my travels and transformation from a hard-driving advertising executive to poet and timeless wisdom coach.

The last time I was in the Big Apple I stayed at The Plaza. I was attending a conference of crack-shot, upwardly mobile executives, whose companies had paid a fortune to send them to an intensive week-long seminar called Marketing Warfare College. Back then, like the big guy beside me, I was a salesman on a mission, slaving for corporate America. *I sell, therefore I am.* Over the last twenty years, I'd come to understand that much of corporate business is run by rabid men with no eyes and that many of the men and women who follow these leaders are good-hearted but confused people struggling to survive in a modern feudal system that promotes only the most fierce and powerful competitors. It has taken a long time for me to come to understand why I had been so driven to become one of the corporate top dogs.

The sales guy beside me, Frank, finally stops his barking and takes a breath. I open a book written by the Dalai Lama.

"Are you a Buddhist?" he asks, accusingly.

"No . . . just bald," I reply, as he rubs his fingers through his own receding hairline.

"I saw Richard Gere leading some march up Fifth Avenue. That Buddhist thing is hot; we're trying to get an angle on it for the Network." I think about how I used to see every person, every place, as a possible hook for some deal I was working. Seeing the pain in his face, as he chomps his way through dinner, I feel a mixture of compassion, disgust, and anger toward this man.

"Don't you eat? You're so skinny; what kind of work do you do, anyway?"

"I write, teach yoga and meditation, and I am a life coach," I answer.

"Writer! One of my sons wanted to be a painter—a painter!" he says disparagingly, rolling his eyes. "I got him straightened out on that! Finished him up at Cornell! He's an attorney at Disney now. Yoga! That's hot, too! Mostly for broads and little brown guys dressed in diapers." The sales guy howls at his own joke. It's been a while since I have been confronted with the bravado of the shadow side of big business. It is clear to me that if this guy keeps up his act, I'm gonna slam him. My mentor has told me repeatedly that I must only give advice, or "teachings," to people when they ask, not when I think they need it. But I'm having a spiritually immature moment, and this guy is a dickhead! I close my eyes, activate *ujjiya* breathing—a narrowing of the throat muscles and esophagus that withdraws the senses, turns them inward, and creates a sound like being in the ocean, bringing you to a state of inner bliss. It does ease the growing anger I feel toward Frank.

A pretty flight attendant asks us if we can use another drink. I order bottled water, and Frank gets his third glass of red wine. As the young woman pushes her trolley away, he turns and whispers, "Bet she'd look good with ole Henry in her mouth. Gawd, I love good-looking pussy." Frank animates, shuffling his belly and groin.

Wondering if he has any daughters, I agree, shaking my head the way you do when you would like to punch someone in the face but manage to contain yourself. *That's it! I'm gonna wake this guy up with a poem!* I open a book of poems entitled *The Gift* by Hafiz, turn, face Frank, and say, "You want to hear a poem?"

Frank bristles in his seat and I read:

> . . . In the overpowering felt splendor every sane mind knows
> When it realizes—our life dance
> Is only for a few magic seconds from the heart, shouting,
> "I'm so damn alive!"

I thunder the last four words in his face as if screaming that the plane is going down.

Frank begins to shake as he lowers his head; people turn toward us, then quickly away. His large frame waggles like a once proud flag. His chest caves—a bully's collapse. Frank starts to look like a chubby schoolboy. I squirm in my seat, take a sip of water. The sadness in Frank's face is deep. I look out the window.

My behavior that day now seems crazy, abusive—blasting a guy with a Hafiz poem about the love of poetry, the love of life. I was the dickhead that day! Like a lot of men I know, back then I was still afraid of men. I wasn't ready to listen to what Frank was really saying—there were still too many of his worst traits in me. I didn't get to hear his pain, his story; but now, after hearing many men's stories, I can only imagine. Remember, guys? Fat boys in the schoolyard, uncoordinated kids waiting to be picked for the team . . . anxious, fragile in the showers, getting brutally attacked by other kids.

Now I am grateful that since the flight to New York I've had the privilege of coaching a few Franks. And I've come to know these fine but hurting men, many of them leaders in business. These men I have coached to become the decent and powerful leaders that they are, have taught me that disgust and anger with another person is, more often than not, unresolved shame and fear in myself.

DENIAL

I don't want to know! I don't care. I don't give a flying—. It may have happened; I'm not saying it didn't. I don't care about Dad smacking Jimmy, the money, or what happened on the fishing . . . About that night, the fight, I don't care about mum. That afternoon, her, my music teacher, forgetting . . . I was home. Sick! I don't want to know, I don't care about whatever happened to Jenny. It is her vagina! I don't want to know! I ga, I ga . . . I got a good job . . . people like me! I'm busy, that's good. Busy! I got a nice house. I got a wife. I got a Range Rover. I'm on broadband, Facebook, Twitter . . . I'm Linked-in. I got a condo in Killington and a house on the Vineyard. I got a personal trainer, a personal shopper, a life coach. I, I, I . . . take Prozac, Paxil, Wellbutrin, whatever! I'm busy, that's good. Busy! I don't care. I don't want to know!

LAYERS

If you scratch lust,
You will find utter loneliness.
If you scratch utter loneliness,
Eventually emptiness arises.
And if you can be with emptiness
Fullness fills you up
Then God walks about
Smiling . . .

CARS

Imagine that the mind is a car.

Are you driven or do you drive? Are you actually seated behind the steering wheel or are you in the passenger seat, the backseat, under the chassis, on the hood, bouncing off the back bumper, knee-deep in mud spinning out, or running for your life in front of the car? One of the first things I do as a professional coach is find out if clients know how to drive their cars, or operate their minds. Many people do not pass the driver's exam.

The choices we make in life are determined to a large extent by whether we know how to drive—that is, are disciplined or are driven. A driven person is headed for the boneyard, whereas a disciplined person finds the highway to high performance and freedom. Everyone must learn how to drive the car they get, the mind they have been given. My car is a Maserati. I'm not bragging . . . I would have preferred a Saab convertible, a gentler ride, as speed can kill. It has been sometimes fun to learn how to operate the sleek thing, but often dangerous and hard. I'm getting there. What has worked best is looking under the hood and beneath the chassis to see what makes the engine purr, and learning to employ an athlete's discipline. When I go too fast, the thing spins out. If I watch too long from the passenger's seat, I get bored. Sitting in the backseat would work fine, but there isn't one. Being bounced off the back bumper sucks, but I have learned a lot about discipline from smacking speed bumps. And as far as running out in front of my Maserati, well, no one can ever say I lacked drive. But the scrap heaps are full of cars driven by pedal-to-the-metal drivers who never learned the difference between being driven and being disciplined.

GOOD

My therapist said one day, "You are a good person, Sean, a very good soul." I didn't ask him why he said that. But I thought about his affirmation for a few weeks. And he was right. I am "good" in the sense that I am dedicated to fully establishing myself in the ground and goodness of my own being. I know the therapist was in no way talking about me being a good man. When I hear the "good man" phrase about a guy, I immediately think, good for what? The word *good*, like the word *love*, has been sentimentalized in our culture. The waters have been so muddied around goodness that often the word refers to a man who will say, "Yes, dear," even before he knows what the question is, or a guy who spends most of his time kneeling at the hem of a seductive woman's skirt, or a boy-man who projects his own God-given power onto some charismatic spiritual teacher. I prefer the rigor of discipline and deep inquiry, not externally imposed but internally tapped and heard and accepted. Being good isn't essential. Kindness is.

OPINIONS

Opinions are like assholes. Everyone's got one. When I offer my opinion, I am learning to speak more gently—thunder and fart less. I've noticed that when I dig my heels in around some subject I feel strongly about, often it is because I am actually unsure of my position, so my mind's impulse is to convince, charm, cajole, manipulate, even threaten in order to mask my uncertainty. Companies and countries do this, too. Big boys boast on the covers of magazines, and leaders of countries drop bombs on other countries. Have you ever noticed how loud such people, such countries can get?

THE CAVE

My client Harvey had disappeared from our men's group and our executive coaching work and gone into his "cave." Men go to caves to hunker down in isolation when stressed and unable to connect with others.

There are many types of caves. One man's cave might be a room his children and wife knowingly avoid; another man's cave could be the endless distraction of nonstop sports programming over the weekend; another's might be his porno Web account; another man's cave could be a drunken stupor of three or four highballs in his chair or working every Sunday at the office when he doesn't really have to.

After Harvey reappeared from his cave, he wrote a message acknowledging his tendencies: "Even though I understand intellectually that life coaching and the meditation group are support structures for sorting things out, when I am in a self-generated emotional crisis, as I believe I have been for the last two to three months, my MO is not to work things out but to withdraw, hunker down, and wallow. So I am reaching out to you to see whether we can reinstitute our coaching sessions and I can return to the Monday night men's group. Thank you, Sean, for giving me the space to reach this conclusion on my own."

What had initiated Harvey's abrupt departure to his cave was that I had offered him a wake-up call, suggesting he was stuck in a pattern of "self-generated emotional crises." In his case, he often felt the emotion in his belly as a nervous tummy. Whenever he shared "my tummy hurts today" with the group, the atmosphere in the room softened immediately. The fact that Harvey is a martial artist, a CEO, and a truly lovely person made him even more endearing to the group. The honesty, openness, and willingness reflected in my client Harvey's message deeply moved me. That is why I coach and teach meditation for a living—to have the privilege of being in relationships with people who have the courage to change.

Although the caves to which men escape appear different, a man's disappearing act always results from a deep sense of isolation fueled by fear. There's a distinct difference between time spent in solitude for rest and renewal, and withdrawal to a cave. The cave is where the mind's claws can do the most damage to a man because isolation kills. A daily meditation practice, on the other hand, teaches a man to self-observe and see exactly how he lies to himself. And sitting with other men in genuine conversation provides a safe place for a man to get honest with himself.

Harvey had begun to learn that he intellectually figures things out, that he perceives through his conceptions of things but does not know the bliss of pure perception. He gets things in his head, but he can't get things in his heart, in his gut. Basically, what a man like Harvey does when he gets frightened is stick his head so far up his own ass that all he sees is darkness.

Conscious, caring men will give other men space to find their own way, but they don't let other men wallow or remain in darkness for too long. Men dedicated to self-inquiry and respectful sharing call each other on such behavior in a straightforward and gentle manner. From Harvey's e-mail there was no doubt he was grateful that I gave him space to find his own way, and I sensed he was ready for change. I also asserted that if he had stayed in the group or the coaching relationship, or reached out to a trusted friend, he would have arrived at his new understanding much quicker than after three months of wallowing. In addition, simply by speaking openly about what he was dealing with internally, Harvey could have supported other men going through a similar struggle.

Unfortunately, in many men's groups if a man shares with such vulnerability, a locker room mentality arises that inhibits men from learning how to trust other men again. Men who know how to be present with and speak for, and not from, the hurt boy in themselves immediately know when another man is touching that sensitive and powerful part inside. Harvey had begun to do this in our group, and his sensitive energy and growing candor with the guys was missed. Harvey had to suffer alone to gain his insights, but suffering is truly optional. For many men, suffering is merely a habit, an addiction to useless mud-wrestling with the mind, which they fall back on because they don't trust enough to live without hunkering down in their caves.

SON

Tossed inside
The surge and seethe of her . . .

For nine months I studied
What her heart was saying:

Kill it, keep it, give *it* away,
So she did!

Forty years later
We met.

Dying in a hospital bed, she said,
"That man from the tenement next door—

"Son, he had the smell of night: a sailor, a soldier, a brawler?
I can still see how that man's backbone bent.

"His dirty toes clutching the sheets; I fought him, I did!
But he shot your future into me, then left town."

My mother grabbed my arm, handed me a faded snapshot.
"As you can see, I was a looker; my dance card was always full."

She heaved a graveyard breath, mumbled,
"You have *his* presence."

– II –

TRUDGING

*There's a thread you follow.
It goes among things that change.
But it doesn't change.*
— WILLIAM STAFFORD

PARTS

"One must not be the part, one must be the whole."
— WALTER RUSSELL

The fragments flail at each other, inside.

Watching as witness, I am amused. It seems there isn't much difference between these parts of myself. They all want what they want when they want it, like spoiled children. Each part is driven by a fear or desire in some form. The prideful part wants my digestion to work optimally, but it doesn't yet and maybe never will. The hurt child wants someone to take care of him. The artist wants more alone time and a patron so he can write poems every day and not have to work at business to pay his way in the world. The poser-artist wants recognition. The scholar wants people to see how erudite he is. The salesman wants to sell: *Homos vendes*—I sell, therefore I am. The performer wants to dazzle (and he talks a lot about truth in art). The victim with the twisted and tucked tailbone and the neck pain just wants the bloody bones and muscles to get along, for God's sake! The empathizer wants people to know how much he cares about their feelings. The tough guy wants respect. The father wants to see more of his son. The student wants his teachers to see how special he is. The saint wants only to merge with the divine and serve. The witty clown wants to make people laugh. The speaker wants to inspire. The companion wants to be married, to learn how to really love and dance skillfully in relationship. The seeker wants to be God, now. It appears that all I am really doing with my life this time around is allowing these ever-changing parts to integrate and dissolve, as if I am becoming like salt in warm water, with feet and a body.

Cool!

HEED

"She just doesn't listen to . . . "

"What?"

"She can't ever hear . . . just won't hear me!"

"What about that bothers you?"

"Every friggin' thing!"

"How so?"

"How so . . . what the hell does that mean, Sean?"

"Let me ask my question differently . . . What about your wife's not hearing you bothers you?"

"I need to have my voice heard . . . I am not listened to!"

"You talk about your wife not hearing you, but what I hear is not that you want her to hear you but that you want her to heed you." A long silence ensues.

"All right . . . I want what I want when I want it . . . busted!"

. . .

Often when we speak about someone not hearing us, we really mean that they are not heeding us; they're not willing to do what we want them to. But honesty stops delusion, keeps a person from trying to make another person the problem. Honesty is the first step in ending the mud-wrestling with our minds.

SUPPORT

Spirit and mind are at war in most of us. The body is the battleground. The Persian poet Hafiz writes on the process of awakening: "It is a naive man who thinks we are not engaged in a fierce battle." When my mind gets muddy my thoughts ping between the poles of memory and imagination, past and future, fear and desire. I can no longer direct my attention at will. I sleep, but I get no rest. Keeping attention in the moment becomes a Herculean task. When I fight my mind during infrequent but pernicious alternating waves of sloth and restless energy, I lose. My mind morphs from merely wrestling with me into a nine-hundred-pound gorilla that drags me down back alleys, smashing my body on the tops of telephone poles. Then I have to pick myself up, slowly dust my jeans, walk back into the house, slump at my chair, press fingertips on the keyboard, and write.

Recently, after such a struggle, the phone rang. I heard a friend's voice on the machine and picked up . . . began to talk about mud-wrestling my mind and how I'd been rattled in my sleep by the skeleton bone songs of dead saints again. My friend asked if I remembered to take out the garbage, which is code for doing my morning meditation.

"No, the gorilla had other plans," I told him.

We laughed . . . brothers-in-arms.

The thing about sharing and supporting is that in doing so we can release ourselves from fear. But as we evolve, as lovely as people are, the support must become an inside job.

THE BRUSH

Bill and I met in Vancouver, British Columbia, an old dog and a wild orangutan. We'd commune over sensitive subjects, coffee mugs in hand at his kitchen table, with his two young sons and beleaguered wife charging about. He'd bark for silence as we discussed such matters as consciousness, the Buddhist void, the witnessing self, God's will, and sobriety. We were good for each other, two headstrong men driving straight for inner peace, unfound. Although both of us had sought recovery and the healing found in 12-step meetings, the coffee clutch and engaging conversation after our weekly meetings had merely teased our souls' yearning for increased depth and reality in our lives. With growing regularity, I'd charge through his front door, having just completed another fast, yoga, or meditation training, all cranked up on this or that spiritual teacher and some new "this is it" teaching. Bill's eyes would sparkle then he'd make a gesture with his hands across his hips, like he was strapping himself into the cockpit of a jet plane, and we'd go at it . . . words, ideas, concepts, questions, and opinions flying around the room like plates at a late-night party in El Greco's restaurant.

We were both self-employed, allowing time to consider some of the deeper questions we were asking ourselves: "Who am I?" "How shall I live?" "Where was Jesus all those years before his short and stormy ministry began?" "Where does my anger come from?" "What work do I really want to do?" "Does lust ever ease off?" "If God is so smart, why'd he create us?"

One Monday, Bill's wife Karen headed out the door to work as I arrived at the house. "Solomon's upstairs, Sean," she remarked, smirking. "He's in the bath, be careful! Why the hell did you go and give him that bloody Bible?" Karen added as she poked me in the stomach. "You'd better start that damn men's group; I want Billy out of my house one night a week, so me and the boys can have some peace. He's turning into a demented prophet! And ask him if there's anything in the good book or his bloody meditations about bedding his beautiful woman once in awhile!" she yelled, opening her car door. Bill's like a lot of guys: when they get into something, they become like racehorses chasing a rabbit.

I tiptoed upstairs to Bill's bedroom, and found him seated upright with his Bible propped on a slat of wood bridging the porcelain edges of the tub, on which were three marker pens, two fat-ass pencils, and a ballpoint pen, fully engaged in the Lord's word. It was quite a sight—Bible open to Matthew, chapter 7, bathwater with wafts of steam rising in the cool morning air, and Bill with a crazy look in his eyes, like John the Baptist preparing the Jordan for group baptism.

"Have you actually *read* this fucking thing? I mean . . . this is the balls . . . the balls! The prophets, Solomon, Jeremiah, Jesus, who wasn't angry in the temple but just laying down the law, man. No more friggin' peddlers!"

"Discipline for the merchants!" I commented, sneaking a few words into Bill's rant.

"Damn right! I mean . . . 'God is love; and he who remains in love remains in God, and God in him!' Now that works for me!" he shouts, punctuating the air with his free hand, the fury of a Baptist preacher in his eyes.

"'For wide is the gate, and broad is the way that leadeth to destruction.' Don't we know that, Sean? Don't we know that one?" Bill continued. Yellow, red, and blue watery smudges marked almost every phrase on the page. There was not much point getting in his way. Bill was on a roll, his mind tracking a burning bush.

I'd given the Bible to him after doing a silent retreat for a weekend with a priest named Father Placcidus, who'd told me that God was big enough for my anger. Bill had liked that comment and asked if I'd lend him the Bible. For about two months he'd been an agnostic trudging mud, seeking light—not that I was much of a Catholic or true believer. Still, we both loved Jesus and were seeking more peace and real male communion—without the peacock strut and locker room banter. Bill and I were hardly new age sensitive guys. We were dedicated to our mundane lives but also wanted to bring more spirit into them and were especially interested in how the heck you weave the mundane and the spiritual together.

Much of what Bill and I spoke about was an attempt to answer that question. "Call more being into our doing, Seanman. That's the ticket," Bill would say with frustration after a long day driving a truck. I'd been going on retreats and considering selling my advertising agency and going walkabout like the Aussies. Since I gave him the Bible, Bill had been prone to calling me at work, and like I was seated with him in his delivery truck, he'd rant on for a few minutes about what he'd been reading and what storm was brewing in his jacked-up mind. "'Be still and know that I am God,'" he said. "He didn't say be good and know that I am God, be generous and know that I am God, be pious and know that I am God, be happy and know . . . He said, 'still.' Like you're always telling me, 'In the stillness, brother!'"

"Right, Bill, in the stillness," I'd reply.

"Shit . . . gotta go, Sean," he'd say, abruptly breaking off the call.

I never knew from his sudden departures if Bill had just seen a cop or some redhead with *the* walk, or just barely swerved by a pregnant woman at a crosswalk in his neighborhood, where he delivered fresh meat and fish door-to-door. We supported each other's insanity, which is what tends to characterize seekers when they first begin the journey—filled as they are with frantic serenity, like moths flapping at the light.

"Saw Karen on her way out," I remarked, sitting on a stool his boys must have used to get enough height to see the mirror and brush their teeth. "She was wondering when Solomon was going to get active in the honey-you're-so-hot department and . . ."

"Yeah, yeah, the rack, I know," Bill said, flipping a soggy page.

"I could always . . ."

"Forget it!"

We talked about the book of Matthew awhile, then Bill grabbed a towel, dried himself, and picked up the end of his hairbrush delicately between his right thumb and forefinger, the way a man might pick up a used tampon that had fallen to the floor by the toilet. With disgust he whined, "Look at this, *my* brush!" There were bunches of black hair wrapped around it the way loosened hair gets caught in the bathroom shower drain. The indignant look on Bill's face prompted me to laugh. He clearly did not appreciate that his wife and boys used *his* hairbrush. I can still see him standing in his tattered bathrobe, Bible in his right hand, hairbrush in the left, red faced, wondering what exactly he had to do to have just one thing in his home be *only* his.

Now that scene in Bill's bathroom strikes me as the first time I truly began to understand what weaving the mundane and the spiritual is really about. At the time, had no children, and my former wife and I were growing apart, as I increasingly wanted out of the mundane world, which in my case meant running a marketing communications company. I did not yet know that wherever I go, there I am—an awareness that came painfully later in my life.

When we first brush up against the fact that many of us are attached to the people, places, things, ideas, beliefs, and patterns in our lives, some of us want to run, others go into denial, and some stay with the awareness but never muster the courage to change. Fear and terror live on the edge of uncertainty, and most folks want things certain, which is an illusion—no thing is certain—and we hold on to things for dear life, regardless of the pain it can cause. I still have a lot of work to do in the area of accepting people, places, and things as they are, but I have learned that often the situation I find myself in is exactly what I need for my inner growth.

It appears that nothing actually happens to us; it happens for us—there is benevolence at play always. I find that when I think I have to leave the mundane world to *get* spiritual, if I open my eyes and my heart I can perceive the Weaver of All Things speaking through many mundane objects, events, or interactions. It can be through a hairbrush; or my son forgetting his winter coat for the third time in one day; or my partner leaving a coffee cup precisely one-quarter full by the bathroom sink every morning; or a driver in front of me who looks like he was taught how to drive in a school for blind midgets in Shanghai; or a teacher who is a dickhead, believing she knows more about every subject than anyone; or the way a certain person's voice makes my skin crawl; or dinner with a mother-in-law who can chill hell. More and more I've come to know that God is in these mundane details as much as in illuminations from deep meditation.

EDDIE BROWN

No man is born violent.

Most neighborhoods, like mine, have an Eddie Brown, whose mom's a mess, has bills backed up, and kids hiding in the closets. His dad can't hold a job, hunts strange pussy, drinks Jack Daniels, Bud, whatever's on tap . . . comes drunk to Little League hockey finals when it's ten degrees below zero, snow-banked up fifteen feet high around the outdoor rink by the river, wearing his tattered black pea coat, cowboy boots, sucking back a brown-bagged mickey. In one game, Eddie's old man falls head first over the boards, splits his noggin, blood staining the ice. In Junior A hockey, Eddie smashes a referee in the face with his stick, cross-checks the guy across the bridge of the nose, pushes the ref's face back into its skull. Eddie gets barred from hockey for life, though he's one of the best hockey players ever to lace up skates. His lost ticket to the NHL spirals into a nosedive of escalating violence, alcoholism, and eventually a life like that of his old man. Most of us know an Eddie Brown—the kid around the corner who everybody was afraid of, a father, a husband, a brother, a son, an uncle, a teammate, a colleague, that lawyer with his Lexus. All the Eddie Browns of the world sit, heads bowed, in the penalty boxes, waiting to grow up, to be men . . . their father's blood spilling all over the ice, bleeding into the world. No man is born violent.

THE IMAGE

A small boy and his mother, head nurse, standing. Uniform crisp, white skirt perfectly in place . . . cold efficiency and absolute order. She's standing on the front porch, hands firmly on both hips, with vice-grip eyes. The gold pin just above her right breast saying: "Don't mess with me, mister. I am your mother!" The image tells the boy who he is, where he can go, who he should know, what he can do.

The boy becomes a man. The man's life is filtered by the image. The man marries, goes through a divorce, and another. He makes peace with his mother in his forties. The man and his mother share, laugh, cry, tease, and give each other support as friends do. But the image lingers. The mother dies. The man goes to therapy. The therapist—a woman—and the man talk and talk about the image. Feelings arise, and the man's body is flooded with sensations. The image grows. The therapist knows how to help the man label and interpret, but the work does not include just being with the image. If he were able to be with the image, the man would see that the image is not real.

It is memory, and by being with the image, the feelings and sensations would dissolve. Unfortunately, the man does not know how to be with things, and neither does his therapist.

The image continues to shape the man, making him a mere shadow of the man he could be. A new woman comes along, but soon she begins to look like the image. The man feels threatened, and he becomes aggressive or runs, or worse, he says, "Yes, dear," to everything the woman says or wants before he even understands the implications. As time passes, women come and go. They like the man, but the man can only see the image, not the women. Instead of being the wonderful husband and companion he could be, the man ends up living alone with the image, and his mother says prayers for him from her grave. Many men live lives like this man, imprisoned by an image.

It can work in a similar way for some women.

A small girl and her father, standing . . .

BIRDS

In my meditations, I used to see an eagle burst forth in the center of my forehead, third eye, with fierce intensity and great beauty. And once, on a morning walk by the Pacific Ocean I spotted a bald eagle perched atop a giant fir tree with regal stillness as four crows flitted about, dive-bombing this king of birds. Suddenly, with a thrust of will he took to warm wind and cloud and sky. The scene stopped my mind completely, so I had no thoughts but was just looking and being. All afternoon I stayed that way, recording each impression my senses gathered upon the screen of my mind, completely at peace and free. Soon, though, my ego began its dive-bombing missions, and I heard the cage door close.

MUD TRACKS

In the beginning love
In the end love
In the middle
Mud-wrestling

CHOICE

In every moment, we must choose as honestly as we can within a field of infinite possibilities. A good friend once remarked about me: "Whenever Sean comes to a fork in the road, he takes it." Earlier in my life I had tried to do everything, experience everything. Until my buddy's astute observation, I had not realized how deeply lust for variety drove me; I was afraid to choose one road as I did not want to miss anything. So I often literally took two or three or more roads at once. This approach can be painful. To use another metaphor, dig many wells and you get no water, dig one and drink deeply. From working with many groups of people and coaching individuals privately now, I can safely say I'm not alone when it comes to the difficulty of making some choices. Coaches wouldn't exist if people could easily make all the choices they face in their lives. People can't choose because they are attached to the outcome. Outcomes are God's business, choice is ours.

I remember a coaching client who said, with stunned awareness, "There are consequences if I make that choice, Sean!" He was young, in his mid-thirties, the pressing weight of choice upon him: venture out on his own or stay in a corporate job that he hated and no longer suited him. We ended the coaching because he never stopped talking about the possibility and was afraid to follow his heart's desire to and take action. The last thing I said to him was a *sloka*, or spiritual thread, from the Bhagavad Gita: "An irresolute mind knows many possibilities." He thought I was paying him a compliment.

TOUGH

The poet May Sarton writes on the process of awakening, "You have to pay for some toughness to walk with a tender hand in the world." I am drawn to men who mud-wrestle with finding a balance between toughness and tenderness. It is ironic that men who understand the power of vulnerability, who are capable of intimate conversation with other men, tend to go only to women for such deep connection; either such men are simply not interested in the jabbering about sports stats, which most men call relating, or they have given up on other men entirely. Expressions often heard by men, from other men who can't bear too much openness and emotion, without feeling like they are going to drown in vulnerability, are: "Get over it!" "You're just too sensitive!" "You got to get from A to B. Move on, man!" "Pull up your socks. Toughen up!" "Oh, Jesus, you're not going to cry, are you?" "Good Lord, man, you sound like my bloody wife!" For every fifty or so men I meet, I am blessed with one man who hasn't given up on his own tough tenderness. Such a man is uncommonly bright, intuitive, fueled by curiosity, dependable, cooperative, and overflowing with joie de vivre. He is a generalist with a hard-won skill set. He has the sense of purpose to build lasting futures. His life force is stronger and more durable than the norm. He is, in a word, *tough*. Not in-your-face army tough, even though he may indeed be a soldier. He embodies the tough tenderness that most leaders fear today, a quality that allows a man to face and integrate his own sensitivity within stable and solid masculinity. I am drawn to men who are both soft and powerful—like water. With them, you can slip in and share the deep water of each other's being, completely unharmed, but you do not want to get in their way when they move in a purposeful direction . . . Flow, brother, flow!

RESISTANCE

The nots in the mind become knots in the body. Most people have limited awareness of how their thinking affects their every cell, fiber, muscle, tendon, ligament, organ, and bone. Patterns of thinking shape our bodies. Take a close look at anyone's body, and you will see suspicion in squinted eyes, anger in a smirk, pride in a jutted jaw, fear of letting go in a stiff neck, a hurt heart in slouched shoulders, bravado in a puffed-up chest, shame in hips that no longer rotate and bend, terror in tailbones tucked under, utter loneliness in bellies protruding over belts, and stubbornness in dug-in heels. I've joked with audiences that "America has tight hips . . . too much bad karma." If we have not made the connection between our minds and bodies, we cannot fully dissolve mental nots and their physical counterparts, body knots.

The pain we resist is stored in the body and leads to premature disease. Research indicates that the average person has about sixty-five thousand thoughts a day. I wonder how many of these thoughts create pain in our bodies. My Svaroopa

Yoga teacher has repeatedly told me that pain is 80 percent fear and 20 percent sensation. As I progress in my ability to let go of merely observing and actually being with what is happening in my mind, I see not only that everything constantly changes but that tracking a thought to its source allows me to sense the thought dissolving back into that source, and thus experience release from fear and desire, and ultimately, the bliss of my own being.

Each of us is capable of living without identifying with or being motivated by fear and desire. But most people prefer to banish pain instead of burning it up in the light of understanding. I began to gain a deeper comprehension of how this works when I turned my attention to migraine headaches. I had suffered from migraines throughout most of my twenties and early thirties. Medical research indicated causes on many levels, but the mind-body connection interested me most. One evening a migraine loomed as I prepared to go to dinner with a young man I had been mentoring. Normally I would have canceled, taken three Motrin, gone to bed, shut out all the light (nice metaphor), and curled on my side as debilitating pain began to surge inside my skull. Instead, I decided to keep my plans for dinner even if the pain made me vomit, a more severe symptom of migraines. I did not fight the pain, or try to get rid of it in any way. While getting dressed, I placed my attention on a spot just above my left eye, where it felt like an ice pick had been thrust into my skull. On the drive to the restaurant, I felt somewhat sorry for myself and so nauseous that I had doubts about my ability to keep my attention on the pain. As we ordered, I observed that my two sit bones softened into wooden chair, then something released along the top of my sacrum bone on the left side of my spine. The pain in my skull did not go away, but was transformed from the coldness of ice to a burning sensation. As my dinner companion shared about his life and problems, I asked him a few questions but kept most of my attention on the pain. I experienced a number of disturbing images as memories rose into my awareness, then the pain in my head disappeared while we drank green tea and ate our sushi. It simply faded away, dissolved without any medication other than the attention and loving awareness I had brought to it.

Since that night, only rarely have I had a migraine. Why? I believe it is because I had to accept them, though such circumstances were not what I desired. Who wants a friggin' migraine right before a dinner engagement or a big presentation or a vacation? I simply did not care to continue my habituated reaction of shutting everything out and staying in the dark until the pain passed. I knew it was time to face the pain. Whatever we resist persists. Some may say, "I meditate, I cultivate a refined intellect (*buddhi*) . . . emotions and pain are an illusion, I'm beyond that." It's true that pain is an illusion. But many seekers I meet use access to higher states of consciousness to banish the pain instead of being with it, and so they never enter into the act of dissolving the pain for good.

The awakening process appears to occur gradually for most people. So start with something small. The small thing I started with thirty years ago was lying on my back on the floor, with my legs on the living room couch, every morning for five minutes before charging into another day of running an advertising agency and event marketing company I had cofounded. Now I do it for twenty minutes, often twice a day, along with other practices.

Master Sri Nisargadata said, "The fruit ripens slowly, and it falls suddenly."

– III –

FOOTWORK

Talent talks, genius does.
— THEODORE ROETHKE

HIRED

"Sean, I'm distracted. People are beginning to ask questions. I'm worried. My father just died, and that's okay . . . er, I mean, we got along okay. He drank a lot, sitting in his chair watching television . . . game shows. We had time to say good-bye. It wasn't a surprise. He'd been sick for some time. I took two days off after the funeral," says Robert, the leader of a high-profile team collaborating on a healthcare project for a prestigious hospital. In this, our first meeting, he explains that, despite all outward appearances of success, his passion and purpose are waning.

"How do you feel?" I ask as he hands me a mug of green tea.

"Tired, I guess. A therapist I met with last week said that I'm depressed," he replies.

"What does that mean? What is de-pression?"

Robert smirks, and I ask, "Are you aware that you just smirked? The right side of your mouth smiled, the left corner snarled." Robert's eyes fill with sadness. He fidgets with his shirt. I sense he does not appreciate my direct approach to him.

"I thought this was a coaching session! I need to get my goddamn goals on target, aligned. Figure out what the hell is wrong with me, Sean. Pull my bloody socks up! If I wanted a fucking therapist, I would have hired that broad last week who said I was depressed," he replies.

"Did she notice you smirk a lot?" I smile.

"I don't need this crap. I don't care if the Dalai Lama recommends you. Perhaps we should end this right now," Robert whines.

"Okay," I answer as I reach for my coat on a dining room chair.

"Wait. God, you're touchy!"

"How can I help you, Robert?" I ask.

"I don't know where to start."

"We begin where you are, not where you are not." I fold my coat over the chair and sit.

"Where I am not?" he asks.

"You're not at peace, Robert. You have a mind that is killing you—a Maserati mind. I know the kind of mind well. I've got one . . . sleek, lean, made for open-road cruising, but the damn engine keeps jamming-up and sliding you off the road, getting you stuck in the mud. As I understand your story, you drink too much, your wife is worried, you tend to isolate yourself, and you work incessantly. Your work drains more than it fulfills—you crank numbers, you crunch data, you craft contracts. You drill down on things. You don't do feelings easily, if ever. You are not at peace, Robert. First, we'll need to slow your mind down so you'll find some inner peace, and go from there."

"This is a little too much for me right now, Sean. I need to get real clear on the return-on-investment here! I'm a results-oriented guy," Robert remarks, his jaw sliding forward and his eyes narrowing suspiciously.

Under stress, fine minds tend to see everything through a filter of suspicion. Some people live this way every day . . . the lines of their faces deepen, they trod, trod, trod, living the life of quiet desperation against which Thoreau warned.

Sitting with Robert, I think of how a thief, when he sees a saint, holds on to his wallet. I smile, remembering the many years I held on to my wallet in front of people sent to help me. It took me many years to begin to believe in good people doing good things.

We sip our tea, chat superficially . . . Red Sox, the Celtics, money markets, how it's hard for him to stand by President Bush while living in New England, and other irrelevant topics that keep Robert suspended from the healing depths of real conversation.

"Why don't I think about this whole thing some more, and we can get together again next week," Robert concludes, handing me my coat.

"I can't next week."

"Going south for some sun?" Robert smiles awkwardly.

"No, just not working."

"What do you mean not working?"

"Well, my son is three years old, and before he was born I'd never worked more than nine months a year. I took three months' rest yearly, laid the field fallow. Now I can't take three months straight, so I take a week each month. I've reconfigured the slow-down time, you might say, but I still get my three months off." I laugh.

"When you were an advertising executive—the president—you took three months off, Sean?"

"Hell, no, I was crazy like you," I reply.

Robert grins. "And now you do?" he asks.

"Yes," I reply.

"No shit, but your clients!"

"I don't coach that week," I explain. "We only do three coaching calls a month, and you can join the Monday men's meditation group, which I make an exception and facilitate most weeks in the fall and winter."

"And you take a week off *every* month for holidays."

"No, holidays are extra. This is just time for me . . . slow, creative time, silence. My colleagues call this timeless wisdom practice, *rest and renew*. It's not always easy. Some days my mind stirs up a rat's nest of stinking thinking. I suppose that's why people don't stop more often—they're afraid to face themselves."

"Holidays are extra!" Robert exhorts. "So you only work nine friggin' months a year!"

I'm halfway out the front door of his house. "Right . . . I can meet with you the week after next to continue our exploration into whether coaching would work for you, Robert," I offer.

"Forget that, man. You're hired!"

SWEET

All addiction begins in the mind.

On my last fast, I'd gone for almost forty days and forty nights without sugar. The problem is that sugar dulls my mind, but my mind *thinks* it needs sugar to keep safe. Safety is my mind's great preoccupation. You can't imagine how many foods sugar is actually in until you read the labels. Anyway, it was day thirty-eight, and I was sailing. Easter Sunday was just around the corner. My mind was so clear that I could give some saints a good run to heaven's door.

Ten years before, I had given up sugar for a whole year. My clarity of mind, inner peace, and creativity were absolutely dazzling. But every time I had felt rejected or unloved over the final few weeks, I'd noticed that I'd had the impulse to suck, gobble, or gorge on something sweet. Remembering this while sitting on my front stoop that fine spring day two days before Easter Sunday, watching the world go by, a part of my mind said, "You know, you've done very well with this sugar fast thing. Down at Debra's Natural Gourmet, they have sugar-free oat bran cookies. I think you deserve one for all your effort." The mud-wrestling with my mind had begun.

"Hell, yes," I think. So I stroll over to the health food store. While headed for the sugar-free cookie counter, I notice the Rice Dream bars in the freezer. And my mind says, "It's okay, they are not real ice cream. Grab one of those, too." I do and pay for the cookie and the bar, then walk outside under the brilliant blue sky. I admire the streamers of white clouds and breathe a God-you-gotta-love-this-world breath, unwrap the Rice Dream bar, and bite down. But as soon as the crunchy coldness hits the back of my mouth I hear that devious part of my mind say, "You're screwed now, buddy. You've blown your forty-day sugar fast, big guy!"

PERCEPTION

Wet, rounded mountains and a brook. Beaver scat. Pear trees that have given their best to harvest. Barn owl hoot! Pond snake slithers. In the garden, autumn sunflowers stoop like wise old men. Wind, always the rebel, casts shadows along the perimeter of the pond and suddenly stirs seven shades of furious yellow. A wooden bench beckons. Sit and sip green tea now, watching a spotted baby turtle meditate on a pebble no bigger than my fingernail. Mind still. Turtle still. Wind smiles. Captivated . . . sink to knees, crawling, grass cold as commerce, amazed in the green beauty and stillness of this garden gem. Is turtle's belly warmed by rock? Does turtle know time? Lifting the edges of turtle back delicately, reverently between thumb and forefinger, I turn my precious friend over to expose its underside.

"Made in China" is stamped on tiny turtle belly.

Wind laughs.

ROLES

Friends, whom I call "keepers of broken wings," were involved in a role-play with me. If I go to their home with a broken wing, then everything goes well. I moan and whimper, and they hold me close, patch me up, and I feel a little better—until the next time. But if I go to visit them with working wings, they become uneasy and appear to not know how to relate to me. They are not aware that they play the role of "keepers of broken wings," although I am aware that I am playing the role of a man with a broken wing.

Awareness is fundamental. We must be aware of the roles we are playing so we can choose more carefully and honestly what roles we really want to play. Roles are how we relate on earth, until we don't. But all the roles we play keep us in cages. When we consciously choose roles, we are free, or at least as free as the role-play goes.

Since my wings are no longer broken, I do not visit my old friends as much. So one day they drove to my house to tell me that I had broken wings. They felt better when they left.

Presently I am floating in an updraft over three lovely willows and a slow-moving creek. I admit my wings get sore navigating certain currents, but from up here I can see other free birds with working wings swoop and dive. I think I will fly over and jive and dive into the Self with them.

ORANGES

I struggled with anger.

So I went to my teacher. "How do you let go?" I asked.

"Let go." He looked out the window into the orange grove in his yard.

"But . . . how?" He stood, reached out to the bowl of fruit on his desk, and picked up an orange, looked at the fruit from a number of perspectives, then dropped it to the floor. I watched the orange roll by my feet. He sat down.

"But . . ."

"No buts," he said, smiling. "Act your way to new thinking. Soft hands . . . open!" He tossed me an orange. I jumbled the fruit but held on.

"Drop!" he bellowed.

I dropped the orange. It rolled near the door.

"You see?"

"You mean . . . just drop the anger!"

"Yes."

"I think I've got it, Master." Feeling a bit like a fool, but a fool with a lighter load, I turned toward the door then felt a thud on my back. "Ouch!" I blurted out.

"Act your way to new thinking!" A second orange rolled along the hardwood floor and settled in a seam. I bent to pick up the two oranges but abruptly I heard, "Leave it there!"

COCKROACHES

People who experience exalted states of consciousness can concurrently suffer from the cockroach effect. It works like this: Although the world can be uplifted into a subtle, sublime reality so that all is well, steadfast, even blissful at times, cockroaches continue to lurk in the darker corners of the mind—hidden but utterly resistant to light and love and still running the show. Cockroaches are the murky and muddy parts of our minds, deep fears and desires that skitter for the dark, hidden parts of the self as soon as the light comes on.

Many seekers forget to clean the darker corners of their minds. They take what Buddhist teacher Chögyam Trungpa Rinpoche called a "spiritual detour," bypassing the hard work of dissolving the roots of hidden patterns of thought, feeling, and behavior, so unbeknownst to them, cockroaches still run their lives. But it is very important, especially for spiritual teachers, meditation teachers, life coaches, priests, monks and swamis, and certain types of therapists to deal with their cockroaches because one of the greatest gifts we give our students and clients is that we are not afraid of anything inside ourselves, so we are not afraid of them.

For about a decade, my way of dealing with my cockroaches was to intensify the light and roast the little bastards in the fire of consciousness. But the thing about cockroaches is that because they have been around a long time their survival instincts are impressive. The cockroaches may disappear for a while but then they come back in much greater numbers until we can *be with* them with attention, firm resolve, and deep abiding love.

Over the last few years, I've learned how to allow into the room a more diffuse, soft glow to adjust my mind's mood. Opening myself to the bestowal of such grace, I have observed a significant shift in my cockroaches. With a softer light, the cockroaches of jealousy, anger, ambition, despair, abandonment, annihilation, and longing to merge with the Self not only refuse to skitter for dark corners but actually creep toward me singing. The more I learn to walk softly and truly listen, the more I hear the little insects. With loving awareness and firm resolve, I am now hearing cockroach after cockroach dissolve, their sweet sounds sinking into stillness and bliss.

INNER STAR

We celebrate, admire, honor, and revere the stars.
Projecting our luminosity onto a star,
That star can quickly burn out
From the heat of our own
    projection,
And we never ignite our inner fire.

We hope to find our radiance in such shining ones.
Born of the sun, we seek
    the sun,
But a star shining only by light and not love
Merely flickers in this cloud-covered culture.

The bright lights of science, sports, stage, and screen—
In the limelight they sparkle, glow, then fade . . .
The big boy boasting in the boardroom, the old
    war-horse,
The once nubile ingenue, the pugilist slumped under
    the bright lights.

Not the light the eye is drawn to the light hidden in the heart.
Enter ever-expanding ecstasy, the bliss of the inner star.
Embody rapture—the timeless wisdom of the Self.
And free yourself in this star-studded world.

REALITY

In the mid '90s, after selling my advertising agency and spending three years on the road living in Benedictine monasteries and yoga ashrams, wandering bareback with a backpack on the backroads of India and Indonesia, I returned home to visit my family. I stayed awhile then bought an old Dodge van, packed the western canon and a few mystical texts from the East into her side panel, and readied myself to head south to tour small-town America. The afternoon before I was to leave, my tough-minded Irish Catholic mother was in the kitchen cooking dinner. I was in my old room, writing. I scribbled the word *identity* on a napkin, then "I am a beam of divinity, animating a mind-body, engineered by a soul, here now." I walked upstairs and handed the napkin to my mother as she stirred the stew, exclaiming, "I finally know who I am!" Mom read the napkin and, brandishing her wooden spoon at my head, said, "You should get a job again, son . . . soon!"

BABY JESUS

I wanted my son to see baby Jesus in the crèche.

We'd talked about the carpenter's kid from Nazareth most of December. My three-year-old son asks some doozy questions: How could he be God's only son? Could he fly like the angels? Why is his birthday on Santa's big day? How come we can't see baby Jesus if he is always here with us?

When I was a kid, I wore out the neighborhood asking such questions, so much so that every adult on Edward Street called me Mr. How Come. I can hear my mother and father rolling in their graves laughing, and thinking, "What goes around comes around."

On Christmas Eve, driving to get my son at his mother's I'm aware of the heavy sadness I feel. This year Beau's with me for Christmas Eve and Christmas morning till ten. The shopping's done. It's just me, my son, and my feelings. I pull into the driveway. My boy jumps in the backseat, bundled, beaming, and breathless . . . ready for Santa's imminent arrival.

No matter how clear I am that his mother made the right choice when she left, not only for her but also for me, holidays can be hard for me. They are even more difficult because I can still make the mistake of seeing my strong emotion for something other than what it is—changing weather.

"What's wrong, Daddy?" my son asks. Not much escapes his attention.

"Daddy's just tired," I respond, trying to sound more cheerful.

"Are we going to see baby Jesus today, Daddy?"

I had told Beau we'd go see baby Jesus after we'd read the Christmas story for the zillionth time. My son's taste for things spiritual is diverse . . . a tiny bronze statue of Ganesh, the Hindu elephant god, rests atop his door jamb, removing all obstacles; a stone Buddha sits on his writing desk, giving clarity of mind; a Zen meditation cushion is on the floor of his room, which he pouts on during time-outs; and a picture of baby Jesus is by his bed, which keeps him safe from bad dreams. He's just recently begun to dream and become worried about safety. So anytime we talk about angels or another god he bugs me until I get him some figure, picture, or symbol of the being for our safety. "Yes, yes . . . we'll go visit baby Jesus tonight at Father Austin's church," I assure Beau. I can't say it is *our* church because we don't go more than on holidays, but Beau knows I love Jesus and talk with him often.

"The reason we can't see him is because he's inside our hearts, right, Daddy?" He presses a mitt into his chest.

"Yes . . . in our hearts," I reply, glancing out the driver's window. There's only a scattering of snow on the ground, which makes it not really feel like Christmas.

"So we're going to see the baby Jesus?"

"Later, Beau . . . please stop!" I hate it when the emotional weather socks-in and I'm in such a mood, but hating it doesn't make the mood go away. So I bring my attention to my breath, feel the heavy feeling in my chest, breathe in and out mindfully. My shoulders let go. We drive in silence, and it begins to snow lightly.

After dinner, we drive about a mile to the church to see baby Jesus. The houses in the neighborhood twinkle with anticipation of Santa's visit tonight. In the church parking lot, Beau leaps from the car, barely waiting for it to come to a stop, and charges toward the crèche. It seems strange that there's no one around.

Walking toward the crèche, I have that warm feeling you get when a cherished memory begins to arise in your awareness. My mind drifts to my father, mother, and three sisters gathered around our cut-out crèche, planted knee-deep in snow a few feet from our front porch, caroling with neighborhood teenagers.

"Come on, Daddy!" Beau calls, as he slides on ice in front of the crèche, tumbles into a hay bale, then pops up unhurt and stares into the scene. There are three wise men riding camels, a magnificent star-bright, a cow, horse, donkey, hens, even a duck and two intrepid mice, but *no* baby Jesus lying in the manger.

You can't really know what a three-year-old having a full tantrum is really like until you've lived through the experience. "Of course there's no baby Jesus. He comes Christmas day, not Christmas Eve," I think in utter disbelief at my miscalculation. You would think that after a decade of exposure to the religious rigor of an Irish Catholic mother and the Confraternity of Christian Doctrine I'd have had that simple fact hardwired.

Now I'm not breathing.

"Where's baby Jesus! I want baby Jesus!" Beau yells, insistently.

"Daddy made a mistake. He comes tomorrow, Beau," I admit, trying to calm him.

"I want to see baby Jesus *now!*" Beau screams in fury. The lungs on healthy three-year-olds are powerful beyond measure because toddlers haven't yet been socialized to suppress fury.

If my son's arms were wrapped tightly around his chest in full pouting mode, I could just bundle him up and whisk him to safety, meaning anyplace where the good people of Concord wouldn't think I was torturing him. But his arms are cutting the night air like slashing blades of the Hindu goddess Kali, as tears stream down his red cheeks.

"Baby Jesus, baby Jesus, now!" he yells again. Across the street, house lights come on, and a car slows to see what the ruckus is about.

I try to grab Beau but slip on the ice and crack the back of my skull, which dulls the high-pitched sound of my boy's angry crying. Finally, I get him in my arms, but nothing can console him. He's totally pissed, and I don't blame him. I feel like a fool in every way imaginable. My boy's flailing away on my left shoulder, screaming bloody murder, and I'm navigating ice-pack as I move toward the car. I try to place him in the car seat but to no avail. Controlling him is impossible.

I'd read in a parenting book about dealing with high-octane kids that when they have a tantrum you should let them expend their energy—not control them, but simply provide a safe container. The suggestion must have sunk in somewhat because I close the car door and watch in amazement as my boy bounces off the backseat repeatedly, then levitates, and throws his thirty-five-pound body from side to side against the car's interior like a rubber ball, all the while offering the world his powerful chant: "Baby Jesus, now, now, now!"

I don't know how long he continues. It feels like an eternity. When he stops moving, I open the door, lift him into my arms, and plunk down on the snowbank in front of the car for a few minutes. We sit side by side under the starry night sky, and my son whispers, "I'm sorry, Daddy." I finally breathe again, and choke on my own tears.

"It was Daddy's mistake. We'll come back tomorrow on baby Jesus's birthday. He'll be here then," I promise, swaddling Beau in my arms. But Beau replies, to my astonishment, "No, he's here *now*, Daddy." Beau pointed upward into the dark night. There are those moments in life, which almost always arise unexpectedly, and no amount of conscious planning could have created the situation I had found myself in. It was what it was, an imperfect father and his son seated perfectly quiet in the snow as a shooting star crossed the night sky.

THE SCOOTER

I'm seated in my car in a Toys R Us parking lot, having a mini-panic attack, "mini" meaning I can still breathe but am jumpy and unfocused. My mother would have called the state "having ants in my pants." I can't seem to get myself to drive to daycare, pick up my son, go home, make supper, and give him the gift I have bought for his fifth birthday—a Star Wars Darth Vader scooter.

Once at home in the living room of my apartment with my son, I'm anxious and upset, although the reason for this doesn't dawn on me till too late. He wants me to *assemble* the scooter. I dump the contents of the Darth Vader box onto the hardwood floor and watch apprehensively as the parts fly out! Some memory presses for my attention. Since my son was born, I seem to be reliving repressed events and incidents from my own childhood. Even though I've gotten used to this, the whole process is eerie, troubling. It's a gift, really, but it doesn't feel like one right now.

Sitting there on my couch, I suddenly hear my father's

distant voice saying, "You've got two thumbs for fixing things, boy." He revered tools and could make anything with his hands. I could do anything with a basketball, golf ball, or soccer ball. I wasn't comfortable using tools, and my dad didn't give me much support for using them. His comments made me feel like an imbecile. He wasn't mean, just not much of a teacher.

Glaring at the parts wrapped in plastic bags and the semi-assembled scooter, I blurt out, "Son, I don't have proper tools for this . . . we'll have to wait."

"But, Dad, you've got tools in the orange toolbox. I'll get it. I want to ride my scooter now!" he insists, charging down the hallway.

NOW, is my son's favorite word! He thumps into the room, toolbox in hand. I'm sitting there trying to get the stem of the damn thing into the front wheel base. "Try turning it around," Beau suggests.

The kid's right. The thing fits.

Then I attempt to put a few brackets together, but a screw the size of a nanobot falls out from between my fingertips and lands in the seam of the hardwood floor. I clench my stomach and jaw and hear myself make an odd sound like a trapped animal dying.

My boy hands me a pen from my desk and says, "Flip it up from the hole in the wood with this, Dad!" I feel an impulse to scream, but instead, after a few long seconds, retrieve the tiny screw.

"See!" He proudly acknowledges his solution and my effort. Then he pats me on the back.

I turn a black plastic thingy that is supposed to hook, and

then complain, "We need to get better tools to fix it. I just can't get this. Get Patrick, Blasé, they can do it. You can ride the scooter next time we are together."

"Dad, we can do it! Look!" my son shouts encouragingly as he points to the picture on the box. "Put it upside down, Dad." I turn the bracket and easily slip in the stem.

At that moment, I hear my father in the room with us, seated right beside me on the couch, breathing but not saying a word, here with his son and grandson, whom he'd never met, who's just turned five and wants to ride his new scooter *now*! I loosen my jaw and a few tears slide down my cheeks.

My son grabs his scooter from me and says, "Cool! We did it, Dad. See! Works great!" He scoots around on it.

Parenting can be exhausting beyond belief. My son utterly fills me up and depletes me on a daily basis. While many parents think they should suppress their old hurts from childhood and get on with things, I've found that such a strategy doesn't work well. There's a healing that happens when you meet whatever rises from your muddy past with honesty and vulnerability—especially right in front of your kids. I sensed that my son appreciated my awkwardness and the chance to help me do something he wanted done. While I stand by the front window watching my son glide gleefully down the driveway on his new scooter, I smile as the memory of my father's harsh words dissolves.

ON THE ALTAR

Stones gathered in the sweet soil of time
Sunset lulled by its rhythm and rest

Silver shaped by an Iroquois chief
Son swaddled gift of innocence

Sandalwood boxed fragrance of infinite good
Quartz sharpened lessons of grief

Angels seated on three sunflower seeds
Companion delighted by the depth of her longing

Candle carved by a cluster of white bees
Christ for his heart is my heart, open

THINGS I'VE LEARNED

A mind that is a light onto itself has no fear.

Personalities are a pain in the ass, until they're not.

Most people operate from automatic scripts . . . my script was being annoyed by scripts.

In relationship, you either vibrate up together or one of you vibrates out.

Most gurus are peddlers.

Choose your teachers wisely.

Love and fame can't stand in the same place.

Mud-wrestling is a choice.

– IV –

A FLOWER RISES

Love or fear, you choose.
— SEAN CASEY LECLAIRE

CONUNDRUM

If you cannot self-observe,
You will never know your own being.
If you can only self-observe,
You will never know the Self.

OM!

Cutting to the inside lane, my tires screech.

From the corner of my eye, I glimpse a fast-moving reddish car and swerve just enough so it barely misses my bumper. Instinctively, I speed up. My first thought is, "What's this guy doing?" The car dodges two others circling the rotary, makes a move past a Poland Springs water truck, of which Mario Andretti would have been proud, and charges alongside my open passenger-side window. I jerk my head to the right and see a fair-sized, middle-aged man who's screaming profanities. The guy's bouncing up and down in his car seat like popcorn. He's way beyond flicking the bird as he waves his fist at me.

"I made a mis—," I start to explain, trying to avoid escalating what looks to be an altercation.

"You piece of shit! You f—! Cock . . . !" he screams before I can even finish my sentence. He's so enraged, he can't hear that I am trying to apologize. I become angry, too, and scream, rolling my window down. The guy stays on me like a linebacker. We circle the rotary outside West Concord, beside a prison, back to the spot where I cut him off. I'm thinking, "Why don't I jam on my brakes, get out, and pound this loud-mouthed moron?" Next thought: "I am a life coach and teach inner peace." Next thought: "I'm glad I haven't yet put that bumper sticker on my car saying, 'Teach peace.'"

I wasn't afraid of the maddened driver screaming through his window like I'd just murdered his firstborn son; nor did I do anything to further provoke him, although I was caught for a minute or so in the old testosterone game. I like to think it was the years of meditation practice or the Svaroopa Yoga, or the body-centered breaks, or the ongoing Kashmir Shaivism sutra study, or the healing experience of writing a book called *Hug an Angry Man*, or the suffering that anger has caused me and others in my life, or the fact that I believe violence of any kind is not the way to resolve arguments that kept me from reacting angrily. But more than anything, it is the prison walls nearby, a stark reminder of where violent behavior can lead—thick, gray cement, twenty-five feet high, twenty-four seven. It is definitely not a place for my son's dad!

I settle back into my body and breathe, slow my car to a near halt, and let the guy going ballistic get right beside my window. I tuck my chin in, relax my shoulders, place my head on top of my spine, lean back in the driver's seat, and beam him a smile and my best bald-headed yoga-face, then blast him with a Namasté hand gesture of peace and a full-volume "OOOOMMMMMMMMMMMMMMMMMMMMMmmmmmm!"

Our eyes meet. His mind seems to settle. The blood in his face begins to flow back into his body. He gazes at me in disbelief, shaking his head from side to side. The Om chant stuns, disarms him. The guy bursts into nervous laughter. Through my rearview mirror, it looks like he's still chuckling as he takes the next exit off the rotary. I continue west to pick up my son from school.

THE DOG

"When I climb I am followed by a dog called 'ego.'"
— Friedrich Nietzsche

Once while traveling in northern India, I dreamt about climbing a mountain at dawn with Jesus beside me. In complete silence, we hiked toward shining peaks, his presence like a thousand burning suns inside my heart. To our left was a great valley, and although it was about a mile away we seemed to be standing amidst its beauty. Willows drank from a mountain creek. On the knoll just in front of us a joyful man in an orange robe somersaulted in a field of wildflowers, surrounded by a dozen gleeful kids.

I turned to Jesus, who smiled radiantly and said, "Oh, that's my brother, Buddha. He loves tumbling with the children." We continued our climb side by side, as the shimmering peaks seemed to pull my being upward into the sky.

I woke up naked, lying on the concrete floor of the small room where I was staying. Soft light filled the interior, as if everything around and in me had been blessed. I was peaceful, happy. The awareness I was given that morning I climbed without the ego, the dog, sustains me when my mind turns to darkness and I can no longer see the shining peaks of truth. And I have come to realize this state does not stay with me permanently because I try to control my life and because I am attached to outcomes. More than that, a nasty little part of me actually still thinks it knows who and what is best for me. During times like that, I let my dog pull me around on its leash.

STANDING IN LOVE

Hip-on-hip they saunter.
Wind writes its way across the pond.
Sun follows—gathering ripples.
Low-hanging fruit beckons.
They step toward the birches.
The curve of her body enters the earth.
His breath intermingles her breath—
Fingertips touch.
She eats him like juicy red raspberries.
He smells her like the stag smells his mate.
Wind finds its voice in the leaves.
Leaves find their wings in the wind.

MORE ON LOVE

Do you love him the way he is and the way he isn't?

It is the *and* that is important because sooner or later the "falling in love" process wears off and the real fun begins. Thank goodness it has been built into the human design that we are capable of the initial delusion of falling in love, because if we couldn't I doubt our species would still exist. I've fallen in love a number of times but only experienced what standing in love is like in recent years. I like the feeling of being on both feet, but certain aspects of my psychological makeup much prefer love as a feeling or a bodily sensation or a thought—love as an idea—where I'm getting what I want and I'm not too disturbed by the person whom I say I love. I continue to observe that these immature parts of me have split off from the Self (love) due to a distorted desire to stay in control or to be right or to think I know what's best in a given situation. Like you, I am engaged in an ongoing process called life . . . learning to love these split-off parts of myself. Ever notice how life tends to place people on our path who show us where and how we hide the split-off parts? And isn't it wonderfully peculiar how these people are often the folks we cherish the most?

I have noticed when I allow space for all of me, especially the disowned parts, then I can allow space for all of you, which makes it much easier for both of us to share our needs, wants, opinions, and feelings gently and clearly, if we choose to do so. And when I don't love all of me I stumble and speak without much tenderness or skill and tend to step on other people's toes. Falling in love is for the young and the emotionally immature; being love, now that is a different dance, which requires two people capable of standing on both feet, their own.

THE TALK

I was invited to be on a panel at a la-dee-da function in Manhattan, a fundraiser for a Yankee think tank. Strange term, "think tank" . . . sounded painful. The other panelists were a Pulitzer Prize-winning scientist, a legendary attorney activist, and a mucky-muck from the United Nations. Our subject was consciousness. I was to give the poet's perspective, share the yogic, esoteric view. We each had thirty minutes to speak, with questions to follow.

The activist was first up. After ninety minutes, he sat down red-faced and out of breath—a passionate sort. The UN official was next. She finished in thirty minutes. Nice talk. The moderator called for a break, and asked if the renowned scientist could go before me and if I'd mind cutting my presentation short.

"How short?" I asked.

"Short," she responded, looking at her shoes.

"Sure," I agreed.

The scientist spoke about the power of the mind and how

his mind had served him. He was in awe of his mind, which was formidable, and other minds like his. He went on for some time while people fidgeted in their seats, then he finally finished talking. The audience clapped, no doubt hoping the bald guy would show mercy, or at least a modicum of common sense, and keep it short, since it was late and they wanted to go home.

I approached the podium. The audience looked weary and somewhat angry. I looked at each person and stood, in silence, for a full sixty seconds.

Then I began. "Desire fires, then impulse surfaces, infuses itself inside sensation, shaping feeling, forming thought. And we think we are our thoughts. New Englanders are a considered people . . . A land thick with thinking thoughts. Go ahead, hone that intellect! In the end, all you will have is a sharper, problem." I glanced at the moderator, her mouth agape. I looked at the audience then bowed and sat down. My talk took ninety seconds, tops.

No one clapped. But as I gathered my coat and papers the scientist approached and said, "You, you, think consciousness precedes mind!" He folded his arms.

"Well, sir, isn't that a lot like the fish being surprised the ocean came before it?"

"We *must* have lunch!" he exclaimed with a mixture of curiosity and fear. I handed the man my card, but have never heard from him. The thing about the intellect is that it thinks it knows but what it knows is insignificant to what it actually is, and could be.

THE KEY

Guru
Is a filling station
The liquid—
Light and awareness
Of your own being
And the shackles you
Still wear.

One night of
Drinking in
Guru's gift—
You feel the key
Settle in your hand
And lightning fill your
Body . . .

You go home.
The light dims—
And the world slams you.
Until the dive inside
Informs your daily life
You still wear golden
Handcuffs

YOGA

Early morning *asana* practice, standing big toe to big toe, naked, balls dangling and tickling the inner thigh, spine loose, up-swelling like a mountain brook, gives a man the sense of eternity. Shiva I am now . . . complete stillness. Head bows. Breath stops. The tail drops, flat bones flatten, and the coiled snake uncurls, throat opens ever so softly. Genitals lean forward, lead the movement . . . tail to cock, cock to belly, belly to heart, heart to crown—crown to the clouds, and beyond. Front, back, future, past . . . no where, no why, no what, no when, no who or the how of it—rising joy from within, and the body turns to Spirit.

THE CALL

If you've ever read the lives of saints, from where many of them began to how they got to where they shaped the world . . . talk about self-centered and messed-up beginnings and perceiving through "a glass darkly," to quote the Jewish tax collector knocked from his horse on the road to Damascus. Consider the skinny, big-eared Hindu kid, later called Gandhi, who was afraid of the dark, a momma's boy, terrified to litigate when he began his law career. What the heck happened to him in that rail station the night the rail steward punted him from the train? Or consider Milarepa, a mass-murdering sorcerer turned saint and revered by millions of Buddhists. Or Mary Magdalene, who was not exactly a reputable young woman. And Augustine, lost in the flesh of whores in Carthage, saying, "Take me, Lord, take me, but not yet, not yet!" Or the pioneering head of the Jesuit order, a former Spanish mercenary. And that other order-founding Christian brother, St. Francis, who gave light and hope to the dark ages, the rich, spoiled Italian merchant's son who had the birds and animals as his devoted friends after he gave up drink, money, and women. Or the more modern saintly man, activist monk Thomas Merton, who "indulged his appetites," as he put it while in college, losing his scholarship and getting kicked out of the university for, among other things, fathering a child out of wedlock and participating in a drunken fraternity party, where he was ritually crucified. And what about Mother Teresa, her private journals riddled with worry and doubt. And some of the Eastern sages and yogi saints . . . The point is: If these wing nuts can do it, each of us can do it. Sainthood is within everyone's reach—as long as you live through the mud-wrestling during the first half of your life, like they did, and open to the deeper call to love and service.

ACCEPTANCE

In awareness you seek not what pleases but what is true. It was certainly not pleasing to discover that after many years of awareness training and self-inquiry my mind had continued to work covertly to impress itself upon the world. My competitive mindset had remained, becoming a fearful, corroding thread. It has taken me hard days and long nights, many humbling years, to fully accept this disturbing truth. My former attitude of "Look out God, I have a world to run" simply no longer worked or satisfied me. Although I thought I was serving and out for the common good, I had merely realized a kind of enlightened self-interest.

Now my mind stops and resets automatically for interludes, and all that is left is peace, bliss, and giggle inside. Why does this happen? I can't say, for sure; my fiery and intense personality has certainly remained fully intact. But in the years before the mud-wrestling slowed down I had steadily stopped trying to impress myself upon the world. I had stopped competing with my fellow man. I had stopped creating prickly vibrations internally, due to comparing myself to others. I had stopped trying to make myself and other people and things different from the way they were, stopped trying to get them to think differently and do things the way I wanted them to. And I became fully aware that life is a game that can't be won, only played. The secret to playing this game of life is to accept what happens moment to moment, to moment the way a child does, and to enjoy the play of consciousness. Now inside there is much peace—a knowing—an emptiness being filled by fullness. I feel free like the wind and the sea, except when I contract into fear and put those darn mud boots on again.

According to a couple teachers I trust, there is much more inside. On a recent visit to such a person at their cabin in the Vermont woods, the teacher listened, we laughed a lot, cried softly some, and all she said was, "Bow, Sean. Just bow more often." That helped.

There is a peculiar thing going on: everything is happening on its own. The "I," the doer who was so intent on taking charge and impressing itself upon the world, isn't. Yet things are happening—oh, so many things—such an immensity of creation going on.

Mud-wrestling is a choice. It ends when we remember and accept who we really are. Then we stop attaching to what arises and fades away, which is everything and nothing. To quote beloved Kabir, "Rain pours down without water and the rivers are streams of light."

ILLUMINATION

Can you really understand?
The Mountain dancing as the man . . .
Alone with heaven's lightning kiss
Of rapture-made waves of bliss?

BEING

Image-free, no thought arising. Feeling completely neutral, not for or against anything or anyone. The body blissful, easy and fluid in motion . . . the cycle of seeking pleasure and avoiding pain, no longer. An infinitely deep appreciation and amusement dawn—the person so full now, everything happening as it happens, in unity with diversity at play.

OLD MAN

Now, the secret to this old Dodge is that everyone who knew me when I was young and dangerous has died. The problem with growing old is you don't think you are old. And with every breath you tend to face memories as fresh as the morning shave. A young woman of thirty-five or forty passes by, with limbs like spring, and even now I want to spread those tender moist petals and get my nose wet—one more time. And, you know how time, fear's mistress, could get so unspeakably slow as we trudged the madness of middle age. All the useless figuring about this and that, how worry was the interest paid and paid and paid on fear. Then time speeds up when you're old. I love to sit in the garden and feel the softness of my own being. Sure, now I ache in the places I used to play. Leonard Cohen said that. How I loved that old dog poet and his dear Suzanne . . . her tea and oranges that came all the way from China. Listen! Can you hear that tiny worm churning in its tunnel, wiggling, working its corner of the garden, opening ever so slowly toward something fantastic yet unfathomable to our minds? Like each of us digging, trying to find our path through the moist, soft earth. Now I sense how important it is to be the earth! And the senses! Taste, touch, smell, sound, sight . . . knowing. Once, I followed the peaks and valleys like a boundless gray wolf. I could smell my way through situations. Now only my hearing remains acute, and an inner seeing, an inner compass tracking light . . . sitting here under the shadow of the oak, listening to the symphony of the willow, the wind finding its voice, strumming her loose strings. I realize that everything I have forgiven has fallen from me like a feather onto this innocent earth, and love grows inside me. And I hear the sunflowers in their ever-expanding ecstasy turn their happy, heavy heads all day toward the sun, all day toward the light . . . I am.

AFTERWORD

Gratitude and acceptance are kissing cousins.

Gratitude is the door to acceptance and ease. Nothing frees me from the muddy pond more than gratitude. I am grateful to be a father, to support my son's growth and development, and to learn from him. I am grateful to be a companion to the woman I am with. She helps me learn the dance of relationship, and I help her do the same. I am grateful to share the sweet warmth of friendship and in-to-me-see with other friends in my life. What they offer is precious to me. I am grateful to be with collaborators in different fields of inquiry—such joy—the act of creation and contribution from others. I am grateful to breathe, to commune with natural things, to be. I am grateful to serve and coach people who care to question how they live, how they lead, and their effect on others. I am grateful to read and commune with the masters, the sages and saints. Their skeleton-bone songs are alive now, if you listen. I am grateful to be awake in the dream, to sit quietly in such immensity, such ever expanding and infinite intelligence and love, such benevolence, simplicity, and kindness. I am grateful that when I look in the mirror I can smile at the man I see.

My own unfolding has been one step forward, two back, one forward, one back into the mud, one forward and a leap, two forward and one back, then two more steps back into unconsciousness and fear, then one forward, a few cliff dives and one step forward again into the light, into love, then one back and ego always forward. Resistance and self (ego) will have dogged me every step of the way.

A human being is an immense spiritual force barely contained in a physical form, a teacher told me years ago. I can't remember who, but if you believe something deeply enough, it becomes yours and manifests. We become what we think. The mind has no choice. It is the finest instrument we can learn to play. Our minds follow the direction of our intention, attention, and will. Love or fear, we get to choose in every moment. I have always believed in love; there was just some mud caked on my boots, stains on my mirror. I also believe that a human life is a great privilege not to be wasted. So walk softly and carry a big hug.

In Gratitude

While writing is a solitary activity, making a book requires a team. I want to thank **Mud-Wrestling's** two readers, my lovely partner Kamala and my friend Lloyd Resnick; their intelligent feedback helped me move forward with the writing. I am delighted once again with the cover design by Dede Cummings and the elegance of the interior page flow by Carolyn Kasper. I am also deeply grateful to my editor Ellen Kleiner, of Blessingway Authors' Services; she holds me to a standard I've come to appreciate.

I want to thank my cohorts at **The SCL Group**: Tony Pelusi, Karen Curnow, Jay Vogt, Laura Collman, Conor Sheehan, Steve Virga, and Cindy Murphy. Our ongoing collaboration and the dynamic way we engage and refine our Timeless Wisdom at Work approach to coaching and leadership development gives me robust intellectual challenge and satisfaction, as well as deep joy.

Many of my initial thoughts, feelings, and intuitions regarding this book were baked during Saturday morning men's meetings at RMOKOS. I am honored to know these men.

And I want to acknowledge the beauty, intelligence, and exuberance of my young son Beau. You my man!

A final note to the reader: Throughout this book, names have been changed to protect the confidentiality and anonymity of particular individuals, but if you think a story or poem is about you it probably is. The work is about all of us.

Blessings of peace and passionate purpose . . .

About the Author

SEAN CASEY LECLAIRE is a speaker, writer, and coach who assists individuals and organizations in increasing their capacity for engagement, inspired performance, and inner peace. Founder of a leadership development and coaching process called Timeless Wisdom at Work, which combines business principles with the ethical discipline and openheartedness reminiscent of monks, he currently serves as president of The SCL Group. Also the author of *Hug an Angry Man and You Will See He Is Crying,* Sean lives in Concord, Massachusetts, with his son Beau.

To learn more about The SCL Group's Timeless Wisdom at Work approach or to book Sean as a speaker for your event or organization, please go to www.seanleclaire.com